Milicent Flick

PIANO • VOCAL • GUITAR

TREASURY of STANDARDS

VOLUME 1 – A to I (I Love . . .)

Mother,
Happy Birthday – We hope
these books will give
you many hours of enjoy-
ment – We love you
so much & hope will
share many more Birthdays
w. you! Love
Ron & Shirley
David & Tina

**MOORESVILLE PUBLIC
LIBRARY**
**220 West Harrison Street
Mooresville, IN 46158
(317) 831-7323**

 **HAL LEONARD
PUBLISHING
CORPORATION**

Home Office: National Sales Office:
960 East Mark Street   8112 West Bluemound Road
Winona MN 55987   Milwaukee WI 53213

For all works contained herein:
Unauthorized copying, arranging, adapting, recording or public performance is an infringement of copyright.
Infringers are liable under the law.

TREASURY of STANDARDS

VOLUME 1 – A to I (I Love...)

Contents

AIRPORT LOVE THEME
(Winds Of Chance)

Words by PAUL FRANCIS WEBSTER
Music by ALFRED NEWMAN

© Copyright 1969, 1970 by MCA MUSIC, A Division of MCA Inc., New York, NY
International Copyright Secured   Made in U.S.A.   All Rights Reserved
MCA MUSIC

ALL OR NOTHING AT ALL

Words by JACK LAWRENCE
Music by ARTHUR ALTMAN

Copyright © 1930, 1940 by MCA MUSIC, A Division of MCA Inc.
Copyright Renewed
International Copyright Secured   Made in U.S.A.   All Rights Reserved
MCA MUSIC

ALL THE THINGS YOU ARE
(From "VERY WARM FOR MAY")

Words by OSCAR HAMMERSTEIN II
Music by JEROME KERN

Moderately Slowly

You are the prom-ised kiss of spring-time That makes the lone-ly

win-ter seem long. ____ You are the

breath-less hush of eve-ning That trem-bles on the brink of a love-ly song. ____

Copyright © 1939 T.B. Harms Company (c/o The Welk Music Company, Santa Monica, CA 90401)
Copyright Renewed
International Copyright Secured   Made in U.S.A.   All Rights Reserved

AMONG MY SOUVENIRS

Words by EDGAR LESLIE
Music by HORATIO NICHOLLS

Copyright © 1927 by DeSylva, Brown & Henderson, Inc.
Copyright Renewed, Assigned to Chappell & Co., Inc.
International Copyright Secured   ALL RIGHTS RESERVED   Printed in the U.S.A.
Unauthorized copying, arranging, adapting, recording or public performance is an infringement of copyright.
Infringers are liable under the law.

ANNA
(EL NEGRO ZUMBON)
From the film "ANNA"

English lyric by WILLIAM ENGVICK
Original Text by F. GIORDANO;
Music by R. VATRO

© Copyright 1952 (renewed 1980) and 1953 (renewed 1981) Redi-Ponti-DeLaurentiis, Milan, Italy
TRO - Hollis Music, Inc., New York, controls all publication rights for the U.S.A.
International Copyright Secured   Made in U.S.A.
All Rights Reserved Including Public Performance For Profit
Used by Permission

Original Lyric by F. Giordano

Ya viene el negro zumbón bailando alegre el baión,
repica la zambumba y llama la mujer. *(repeat)*

Tengo gana de bailar el nuevo compas.
Dicen todos cuando me veen pasar:
Chica, donde vas? Me voy pa' bailá el baión.
Tengo gana de bailar el nuevo compas.
Dicen todos cuando me veen pasar:
Chica, donde vas? Me voy pa' bailá el baión.

THE ANNIVERSARY WALTZ

Words and Music by AL DUBIN
& DAVE FRANKLIN

Copyright © 1941 by Mayfair Music Corp.
Copyright Renewed, controlled by Chappell & Co., Inc. (Intersong Music, Publisher) in the U.S.A. only
International Copyright Secured   ALL RIGHTS RESERVED   Printed in the U.S.A.
Unauthorized copying, arranging, adapting, recording or public performance is an infringement of copyright.
Infringers are liable under the law.

ANOTHER OP'NIN', ANOTHER SHOW

(From "KISS ME, KATE")

Words and Music by
COLE PORTER

Copyright © 1949 by Cole Porter
Copyright renewed, assigned to John F. Wharton, Trustee of the Cole Porter Musical & Literary Property Trusts
Chappell & Co., Inc., owner of publication and allied rights throughout the World.
International Copyright Secured   ALL RIGHTS RESERVED   Printed in the U.S.A.
Unauthorized copying, arranging, adapting, recording or public performance is an infringement of copyright.
Infringers are liable under the law.

(HEY, WON'T YOU PLAY)
ANOTHER SOMEBODY DONE SOMEBODY WRONG SONG

Words and Music by LARRY BUTLER
and CHIPS MOMAN

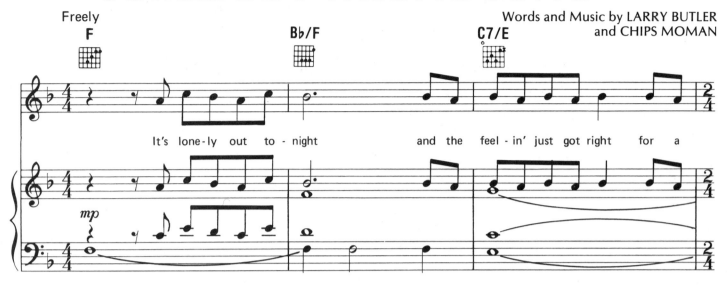

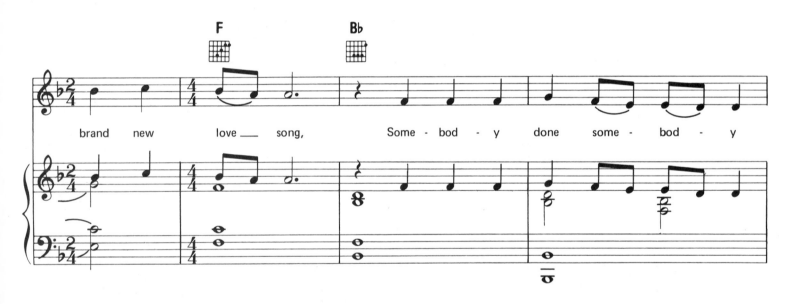

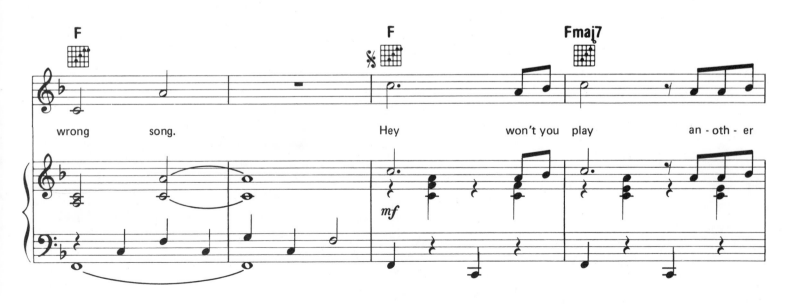

Copyright © 1975 by Tree Publishing Co., Inc. and Screen Gems-EMI Music, Inc., 8 Music Square West, Nashville, TN 37203
This arrangement Copyright © 1975 by Tree Publishing Co., Inc. and Screen Gems-EMI Music, Inc.
International Copyright Secured   Made in U.S.A.   All Rights Reserved

BABY FACE

Words and Music by E
and HARRY AKST

© 1926 WARNER BROS. INC.
Copyright Renewed
All Rights Reserved

ARE YOU LONESOME TONIGHT?

Words and Music by ROY TURK
and LOU HANDMAN

TRO - © Copyright 1926 and renewed 1956 and 1984 Cromwell Music, Inc. and Bourne Co., New York, NY
International Copyright Secured   Made in U.S.A.
All Rights Reserved Including Public Performance For Profit
Used by Permission

AROUND THE WORLD

Words and Music by VICTOR YOUNG
and HAROLD ADAMSON

Copyright © 1956 by Victor Young Publications, Inc.
Copyright Renewed, Assigned to Chappell & Co., Inc. and Liza Music Corp.
International Copyright Secured   ALL RIGHTS RESERVED   Printed in the U.S.A.
Unauthorized copying, arranging, adapting, recording or public performance is an infringement of copyright.
Infringers are liable under the law.

As Long As He Needs Me

(From the Columbia Pictures - Romulus film "OLIVER!")

Words and Music by LIONEL BART

© Copyright 1960 Lakeview Music Co., Ltd., London, England
TRO-Hollis Music, Inc., New York, controls all publication rights for the U.S.A. and Canada
International Copyright Secured   Made in U.S.A.
All Rights Reserved Including Public Performance For Profit
Used by Permission

BABY, WON'T YOU PLEASE COME HOME

Words and Music by CHARLES WARFIELD
and CLARENCE WILLIAMS

© Copyright 1919 by MCA MUSIC, A Division of MCA Inc., New York, NY
Copyright Renewed
International Copyright Secured   Made in U.S.A.   All Rights Reserved
MCA MUSIC

BAKER STREET

Words and Music by
GERRY RAFFERTY

Copyright © 1978 by Rafferty Songs Limited
All rights administered for the U.S. and Canada by Hudson Bay Music, Inc.
International Copyright Secured   Made in U.S.A.   All Rights Reserved
Used by Permission

Verse 3:   Way down the street there's a lot in his place,
            He opens his door he's got that look on his face
            And he asks you where you've been
            You tell him who you've seen and you talk about anything.

Verse 4:   He's got this dream about buyin' some land he's gonna
            Give up the booze and the one night stands and
            Then you'll settle down with some quiet little town
            And forget about everything.

Chorus 3:   But you know you'll always keep movin'
            You know he's never gonna stop movin'
            'Cause he's rollin' he's the rollin' stone.

Chorus 4:   When you wake up it's a new mornin'
            The sun is shinin', it's a new mornin'
            And you're goin', you're goin' home.

THE BEST THINGS IN LIFE ARE FREE

Music and Lyrics by B.G. DeSYLVA,
LEW BROWN and RAY HENDERSON

Copyright © 1927 by DeSylva, Brown and Henderson, Inc.
Copyright Renewed, assigned to Chappell & Co., Inc.
International Copyright Secured   ALL RIGHTS RESERVED   Printed in the U.S.A.
Unauthorized copying, arranging, adapting, recording or public performance is an infringement of copyright.
Infringers are liable under the law.

BEWITCHED
(From "PAL JOEY")

Words by LORENZ HART
Music by RICHARD RODGERS

Moderately, in 2

He's a fool and don't I know it. But a fool can have his charms.
Love's the same old sad sen - sa - tion. Late - ly I've not slept a wink

I'm in love and don't I show it, Like a babe in arms.
Since this half - pint im - i - ta - tion

Put me on the blink. I'm wild a - gain, Be - guiled a - gain, A

Copyright © 1941 by Chappell & Co., Inc.
Copyright Renewed
International Copyright Secured   ALL RIGHTS RESERVED   Printed in the U.S.A.
Unauthorized copying, arranging, adapting, recording or public performance is an infringement of copyright.
Infringers are liable under the law.

BLUESETTE

Words by NORMAN GIMBEL
Music by JEAN THIELEMANS

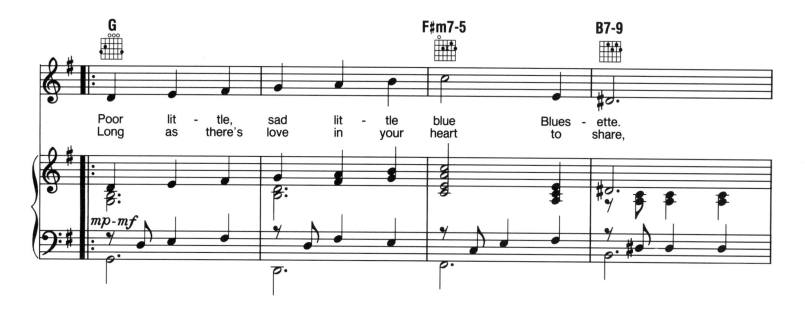

Poor lit - tle, sad lit - tle blue Blues - ette.
Long as there's love lit in your heart Blues to share,

Don't you cry, don't you fret.
dear Blues - ette, don't des - pair.

© Copyright 1963, 1964 by MUSIC CORPORATION OF AMERICA, INC., New York, NY
Rights Administered by MCA MUSIC, A Division of MCA Inc., New York, NY
International Copyright Secured   Made in U.S.A.   All Rights Reserved

MCA MUSIC

48

(From Walt Disney's "CINDERELLA")

BIBBIDI-BOBBIDI-BOO
(THE MAGIC SONG)

Words by JERRY LIVINGSTON
Music by MACK DAVID and AL HOFFMAN

©1948 WALT DISNEY MUSIC COMPANY
Copyright Renewed
International Copyright Secured   Made in U.S.A.   All Rights Reserved

BLUE VELVET

Words and Music by BERNIE WAYNE
and LEE MORRIS

Copyright © 1951 Vogue Music (c/o The Welk Music Group, Santa Monica, CA 90401) Copyright renewed.
International Copyright Secured   Made in U.S.A.   All Rights Reserved

BOO-HOO

Words and Music by EDWARD HEYMAN,
CARMEN LOMBARDO and JOHN JACOB LOEB

© 1936 SHAPIRO, BERNSTEIN & CO., INC.
© Renewed 1964 FRANK MUSIC CORP.
International Copyright Secured   Made in U.S.A.   All Rights Reserved

BROKEN-HEARTED MELODY

Words by HAL DAVID
Music by SHERMAN EDWARDS

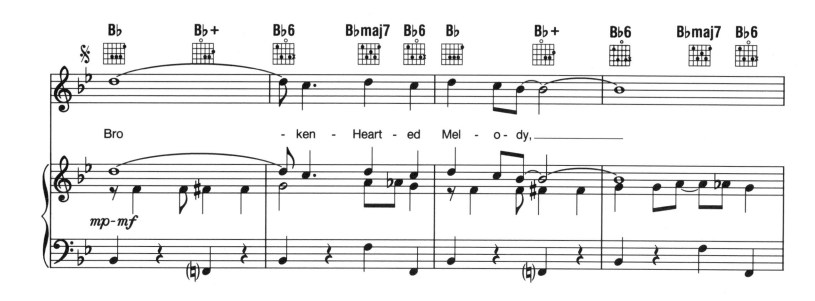

Bro - ken - Heart - ed Mel - o - dy,

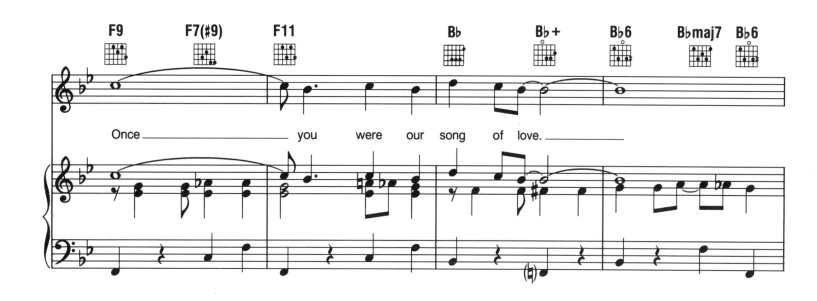

Once you were our song of love.

© 1959 WAROCK CORP.
International Copyright Secured   Made in U.S.A.   All Rights Reserved

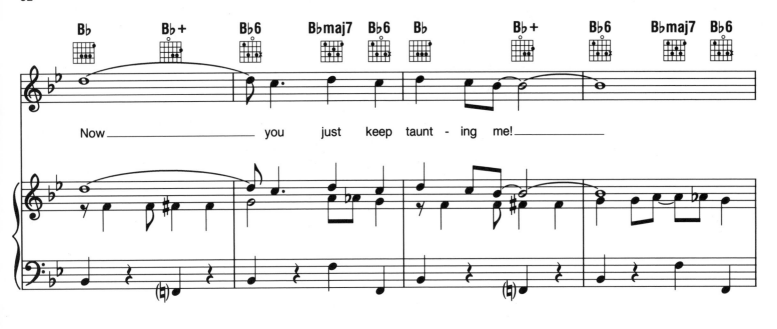

Now_____ you just keep taunt - ing me!___

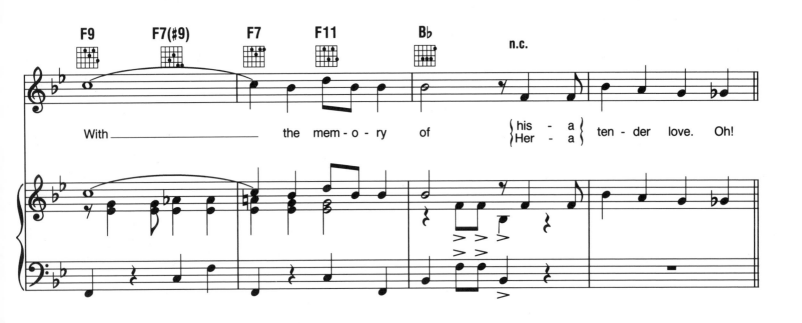

With_____ the mem-o-ry of {his - a / Her - a} ten - der love. Oh!

Bro - ken Heart - ed Mel - o - dy,__ Must you keep re - mind-ing me,__

Bro - ken Heart - ed Mel - o - dy,__ That {he / she} used to sing to me,__

Bro - ken Heart - ed Mel - o - dy,__ Won't you bring {him / her} back to me?__

BOOGIE WOOGIE BUGLE BOY

Words and Music by DON RICE
and HUGHIE PRINCE

Medium Boogie Woogie

He was a fa - mous trum - pet man from out Chi -

ca - go way, ___ He had a "boo - gie" style that no one

else could play. ___ He was the top man of his craft

© Copyright 1940, 1941 by MCA MUSIC, A Division of MCA Inc., New York, NY
Copyright Renewed
International Copyright Secured   Made in U.S.A.   All Rights Reserved

MCA MUSIC

BUTTON UP YOUR OVERCOAT

Words and Music by B.G. DeSYLVA,
LEW BROWN and RAY HENDERSON

Copyright © 1928 by DeSylva, Brown & Henderson
Copyright Renewed, assigned to Chappell & Co., Inc.
International Copyright Secured   ALL RIGHTS RESERVED   Printed in the U.S.A.
Unauthorized copying, arranging, adapting, recording or public performance is an infringement of copyright.
Infringers are liable under the law.

BLUE PRELUDE

Words by GORDON JENKINS
Music by JOE BISHOP

Copyright © 1933 by ISHAM JONES
Copyright Assigned 1944 to WORLD MUSIC, INC.
Copyright Renewed

C'EST SI BON
(It's So Good)

English Words by JERRY SEELEN
French Words by ANDRE HORNEZ
Music by HENRI BETTI

© Copyright 1947, 1949, 1950 by Arpege Editions Musicales, France
Sole Selling Agent MCA MUSIC, a division of MCA Inc., 445 Park Avenue, New York, N.Y. for U.S.A. & Canada
International Copyright Secured   Made in U.S.A.   All Rights Reserved

MCA MUSIC

C'EST MAGNIFIQUE
(From "CAN-CAN")

Words and Music by
COLE PORTER

*Pronounced "say man-yee-fee-kuh"

Copyright © 1952, 1953 by Cole Porter
Copyright renewed, assigned to Robert H. Montgomery, Trustee of the Cole Porter Musical and Literary Property Trusts
Chappell & Co., Inc., Publisher
International Copyright Secured   ALL RIGHTS RESERVED   Printed in the U.S.A.
Unauthorized copying, arranging, adapting, recording or public performance is an infringement of copyright.
Infringers are liable under the law.

CALDONIA
(WHAT MAKES YOUR BIG HEAD SO HARD?)

Words and Music by
FLEECIE MOORE

Medium boogie woogie tempo

© 1945 CHERIO CORP.
© Renewed 1973 CHERIO CORP.
International Copyright Secured   Made in U.S.A.   All Rights Reserved

don- ia! __ Cal - don- ia! __ What Makes Your Big Head So Hard?

CALIFORNIA DREAMIN'

Words and Music by JOHN PHILLIPS

Medium Rock beat

© Copyright 1965 by MCA Music, A Division of MCA, Inc., New York
International Copyright Secured   Made in U.S.A.   All Rights Reserved

MCA MUSIC

CANDLE ON THE WATER

(From Walt Disney Productions' "PETE'S DRAGON")

Words and Music by AL KASHA
and JOEL HIRSCHHORN

© 1976 WALT DISNEY MUSIC COMPANY and WONDERLAND MUSIC CO., INC.
International Copyright Secured   Made in U.S.A.   All Rights Reserved

CALL ME

Moderately

Words and Music by TONY HATCH

If you're feel-ing sad and lone-ly, there's a ser-vice I ____ can ren-der,

Tell the one who loves ____ you on-ly, I can be so warm ____ and ten-der.

Call me! ____ Don't be a-fraid; ____ you can call me. ____ May-be it's late, ____ but just

© Copyright 1965 by Welbeck Music Ltd., London, England
Sole Selling Agent DUCHESS MUSIC CORPORATION (MCA), New York, NY for the U.S.A. and Canada
International Copyright Secured   Made in U.S.A.   All Rights Reserved

MCA MUSIC

CAMELOT
(From "CAMELOT")

Words by ALAN JAY LERNER
Music by FREDERICK LOEWE

Copyright © 1960, 1961 by Alan Jay Lerner and Frederick Loewe
Chappell & Co., Inc., owner of publication and allied rights throughout the World
International Copyright Secured   ALL RIGHTS RESERVED   Printed in the U.S.A.
Unauthorized copying, arranging, adapting, recording or public performance is an infringement of copyright.
Infringers are liable under the law.

CAN'T HELP LOVIN' DAT MAN

Words by OSCAR HAMMERSTEIN II
Music by JEROME KERN

Copyright © 1927 T.B. Harms Company (c/o The Welk Music Group, Santa Monica, CA 90401) Copyright Renewed.
International Copyright Secured   Made in U.S.A.   All Rights Reserved

CANDY

Words and Music by MACK DAVID,
JOAN WHITNEY and ALEX KRAMER

Moderately slow

Copyright © 1944 Leo Feist, Inc
Copyright renewed and assigned to Harry Von Tilzer Music Publishing Company and Kramer-Whitney, Inc.
(c/o The Welk Music Group, Santa Monica, Calif. 90401)
International Copyright Secured.   All rights reserved.
Used by permission.

CARA MIA

Words and Music by
TULIO TRAPANI & LEE LANGE

Moderately

Ca - ra Mi - a why must we say good - bye?

Each time we part, my heart wants to die. My

dar - ling hear my pray'r, Ca - ra Mi - a fair Here are my

© 1954 LEO FEIST, INC.
Copyright Renewed 1982
Copyright Renewal Proprietor SEPTEMBER MUSIC CORP.
Rights for the U.S.A. controlled by SEPTEMBER MUSIC CORP.
Rights for the rest of the world controlled by LEO FEIST, INC.
All Rights of LEO FEIST, INC. Assigned to CBS CATALOGUE PARTNERSHIP
All Rights of LEO FEIST, INC. Controlled and Administered by CBS FEIST CATALOG, INC.
International Copyright Secured   All Rights Reserved

CHANSON D'AMOUR
(SONG OF LOVE)
The Ra-Da-Da-Da-Da Song

Words and Music by WAYNE SHANKLIN

Copyright © 1958 Bibo Music Publishers (c/o The Welk Music Group, Santa Monica, CA 90401)
International Copyright Secured   Made in U.S.A.   All Rights Reserved

CHIM CHIM CHER-EE

(From Walt Disney's "MARY POPPINS")

Words and Music by
RICHARD M. SHERMAN
and ROBERT B. SHERMAN

Lightly, with gusto

Chim chim-in-ey, chim chim-in-ey, chim chim cher-ee! A sweep is as

luck-y, as luck-y can be. Chim chim-in-ey, chim chim-in-ey,

chim chim cher-oo! Good luck will rub off when I shakes 'ands with

© 1963 WONDERLAND MUSIC CO., INC.
International Copyright Secured   Made in U.S.A.   All Rights Reserved

COME BACK TO ME
(From "ON A CLEAR DAY YOU CAN SEE FOREVER")

Words by ALAN JAY LERNER
Music by BURTON LANE

Copyright © 1965 by Alan Jay Lerner & Burton Lane
Chappell & Co., Inc., owner of publication and allied rights throughout the World
International Copyright Secured   ALL RIGHTS RESERVED   Printed in the U.S.A.
Unauthorized copying, arranging, adapting, recording or public performance is an infringement of copyright.
Infringers are liable under the law.

CONSIDER YOURSELF

(From the Musical "OLIVER!")

Words and Music by
LIONEL BART

© Copyright 1960 LAKEVIEW MUSIC CO., LTD., London, England
TRO - HOLLIS MUSIC, INC., New York, controls all publication rights for the U.S.A., and Canada
International Copyright Secured   Made in U.S.A.
All Rights Reserved Including Public Performance For Profit
Used by Permission

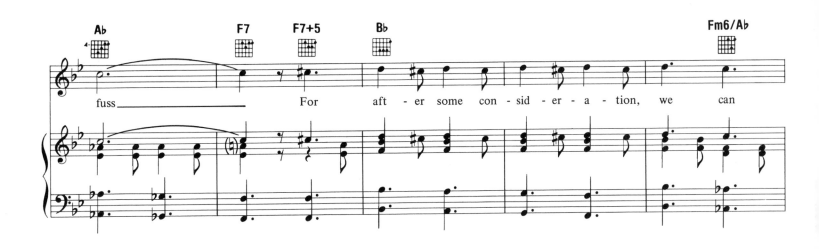

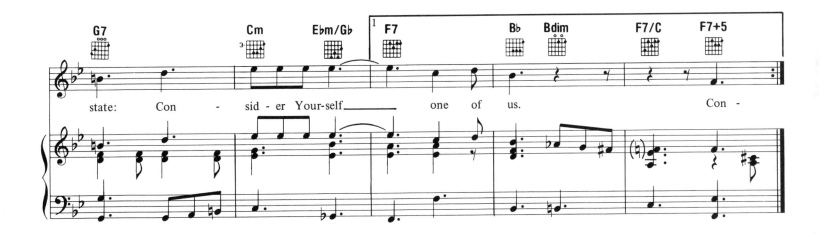

COULD I HAVE THIS DANCE

Words and Music by WAYLAND HOLYFIELD
and BOB HOUSE

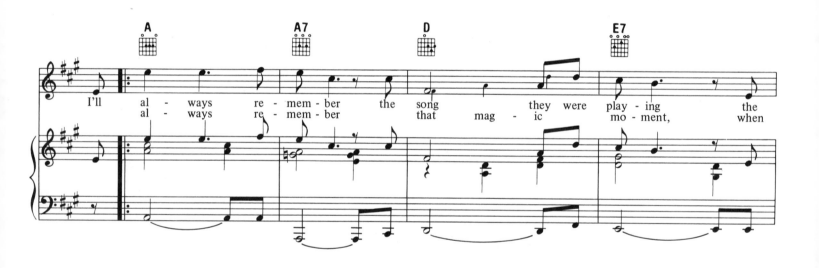

I'll al - ways re - mem - ber the song they were play - ing the
al - ways re - mem - ber that mag - ic mo - ment, when

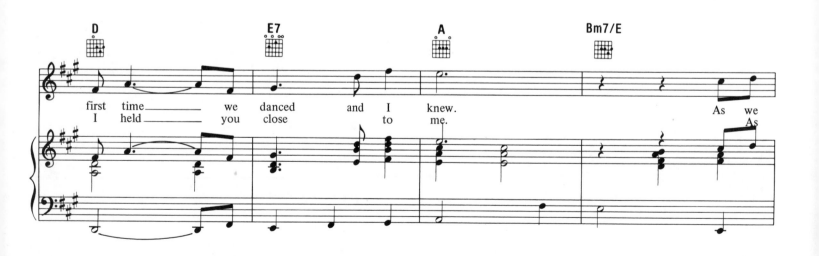

first time_____ we danced and I knew.
I held_____ you close to me. As we

As we

Copyright © 1980 by Bibo Music Publishers (c/o The Welk Music Group, Santa Monica, CA 90401) and
Tree Publishing Co., Inc., 8 Music Square West, Nashville, TN 37203
This arrangement Copyright © 1983 by Bibo Music Publishers and Tree Publishing Co., Inc.
International Copyright Secured   Made in U.S.A.   All Rights Reserved

120

DADDY DON'T YOU WALK SO FAST

Words by PETER CALLANDER
Music by GEOFF STEPHENS

Casually

Copyright © 1970 DICK JAMES MUSIC S.A.
Assigned to DICK JAMES MUSIC, LTD., James House, 5 Theobald's Road, London WC1X 8SE, England for the world.
All rights for the United States and Canada controlled by DICK JAMES MUSIC, INC., 24 Music Square East, Nashville, TN 37203
International Copyright Secured   Made in U.S.A.   All Rights Reserved

122

DADDY

Words and Music by
Bob Troup

Medium bounce tempo

VOICE

Hey! lis - ten to my sto - ry 'bout_ a gal named Dai - sy Mae_ La - zy Dai - sy Mae_

Copyright © 1941 by REPUBLIC MUSIC CORP.
Copyright Assigned 1961 to WORLD MUSIC, INC.
Copyright Renewed
International Copyright Secured   Made in U.S.A.   All Rights Reserved

Her dis-po - si - tion   is ra-ther sweet and charm-ing;

At times a - larm - ing.   So— they say. _____

(Interlude)

She had a

man rich, tall, dark, hand-some large and strong to whom she used to sing this song:

DINAH

Words by SAM M. LEWIS and JOE YOUNG
Music by HARRY AKST

Copyright © 1925 B & G AKST PUBLISHING CO.
Pursuant to Sections 304(c) and 401(b) of the U.S. Copyright Law.
International Copyright Secured   All Rights Reserved

DO I HEAR A WALTZ?

(From "DO I HEAR A WALTZ?")

Music by Richard Rodgers
Lyrics by Stephen Sondheim

Copyright © 1965 by Richard Rodgers & Stephen Sondheim
Williamson Music Co. & Burthen Music Co., Inc., owner of publication and allied rights throughout the world.
Chappell & Co., Inc., sole selling agent.
International Copyright Secured   ALL RIGHTS RESERVED   Printed in the U.S.A.
Unauthorized copying, arranging, adapting, recording or public performance is an infringement of copyright.
Infringers are liable under the law.

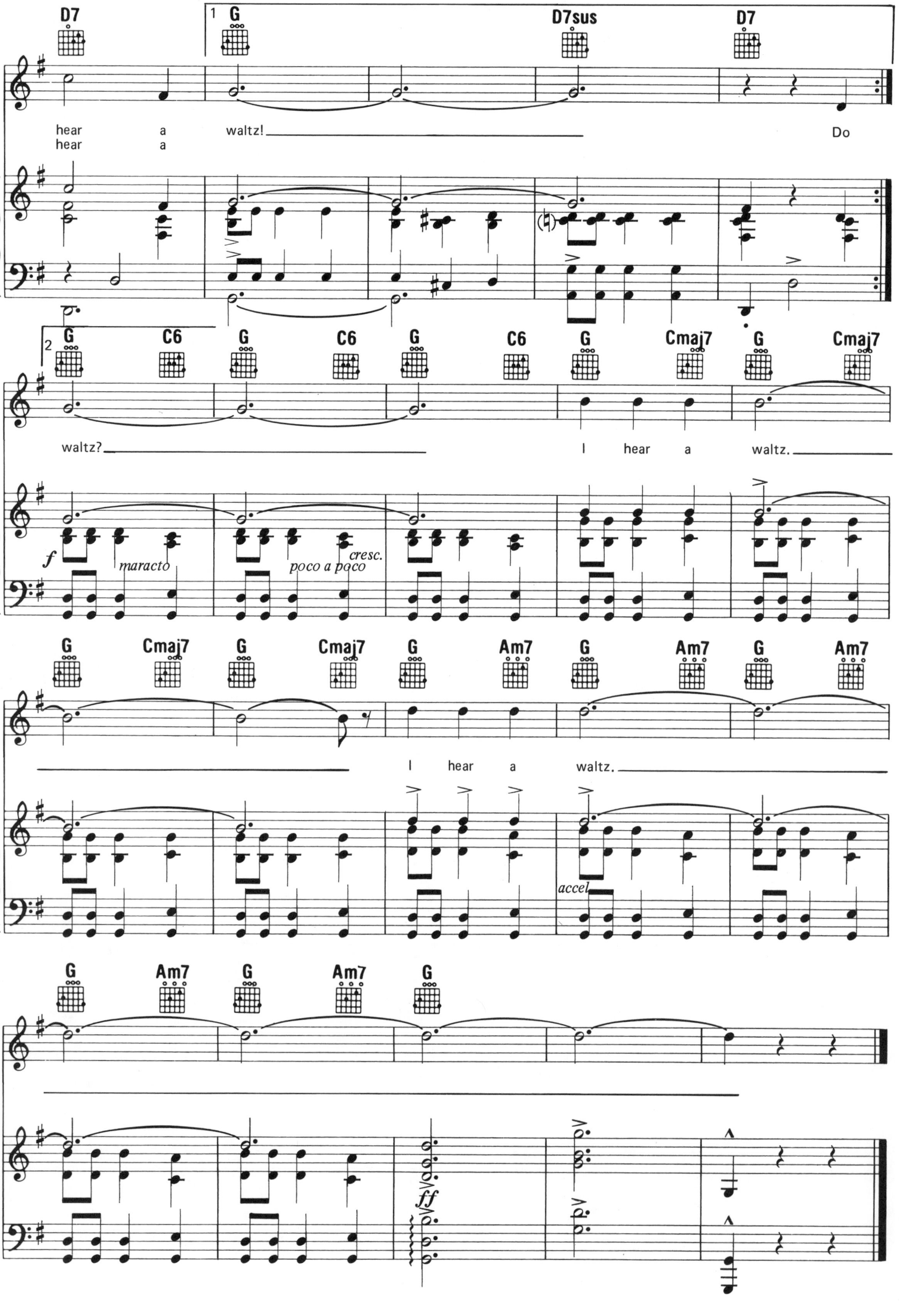

D7
G
D7sus
D7
hear a waltz!
Do
hear a
G C6 G C6 G C6 G Cmaj7 G Cmaj7
waltz?
I hear a waltz.
f
maracto
poco a poco
cresc.
G Cmaj7 G Cmaj7 G Am7 G Am7 G Am7
I hear a waltz.
accel
G Am7 G Am7 G
ff

DOMINO

English Words by DON RAYE
French Words by JACQUES PLANTE
Music by LOUIS FERRARI

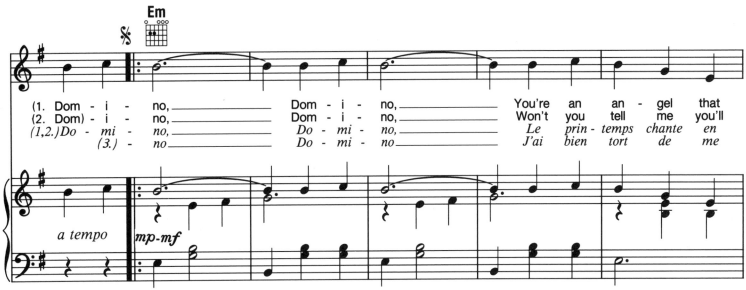

© Copyright 1950, 1956, 1968 by Arpege Editions Musicales, Paris, France. Copyright Renewed.
Sole Selling Agent MCA MUSIC, A Division of MCA Inc., New York, NY
International Copyright Secured   Made in U.S.A.   All Rights Reserved

MCA MUSIC

Slightly faster (ad lib)

B7   ¹ Em   Optional repeat   ² Em   Em

To Coda

cry, Dom - i - no?   Dom - i   no.   Just one look in your
I, Dom - i -
mée Do - mi - no.   plus.   1. Mê - fie - toi, mon a -
ger, moi non   2. Il est u - ne pen -

mf   mp

D   Am   B   Em   D   Am

eyes and I melt waith de - sire, Just a touch of your hands and I burst in - to
mour, je t'ai trop par - don - né J'ai per - du plus de nuits que tu m'en as don
sée que je ne souf - fre pas C'est qu'on puis - se me pren - dre ma place en tes

B   F♯m7   B7   E   B7

fire. And my whole world ___ fills with mu - sic, ___ When I'm lost in
nées. Bien plus d'heu - res ___ A t'at ten - dre, ___ Qu'à te pre - dre ___
bras. Je sup - por - te ___ Bien des cho - ses, ___ Mais a for - ce,

a tempo

DON'T CRY FOR ME ARGENTINA
(From the opera "EVITA")

Lyric by TIM RICE
Music by ANDREW LLOYD WEBBER

© Copyright 1976, 1977 by Evita Music Ltd., London, England
Sole Selling Agent MCA MUSIC, A Division of MCA, Inc., New York, NY for the Entire Western Hemisphere.
International Copyright Secured   Made in U.S.A.   All Rights Reserved

MCA MUSIC

142

all you have to do is look at me to know that ev-'ry word is true.

DON'T SLEEP IN THE SUBWAY

Words and Music by TONY HATCH
and JACKIE TRENT

Medium beat

You wan-der a-round___ on your own___ lit-tle cloud___ When you
You try to be smart___ then you take___ it to heart___ 'Cause it

don't see the why or the where - fore___
hurts when your e - go's de - fla - ted___

You walk out on me___ when we both___ dis - a - gree___ 'Cause to
You don't re - a - lise___ that it's all___ com-pro - mise___ And the

© Copyright 1967 by Welbeck Music Ltd., London, England
Sole Selling Agent MCA MUSIC, A Division of MCA Inc., New York, NY
International Copyright Secured   Made in U.S.A.   All Rights Reserved

MCA MUSIC

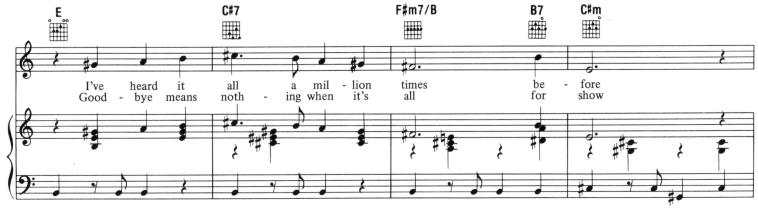

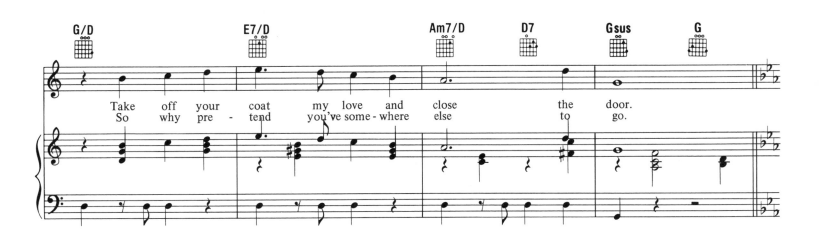

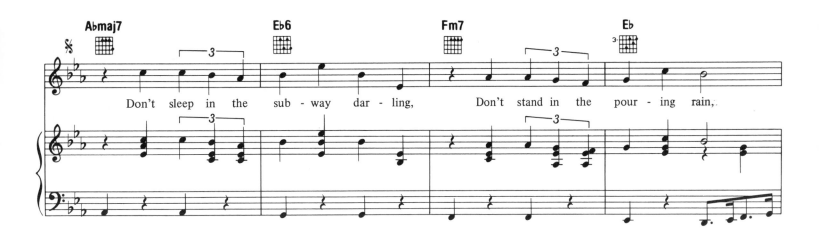

DOWN AMONG THE SHELTERING PALMS

Words by JAMES BROCKMAN
Music by ABE OLMAN

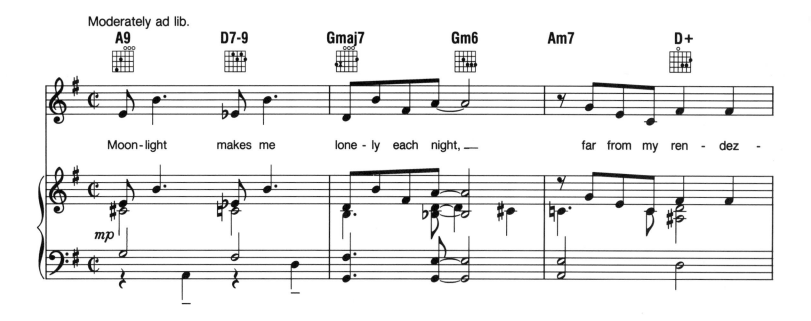

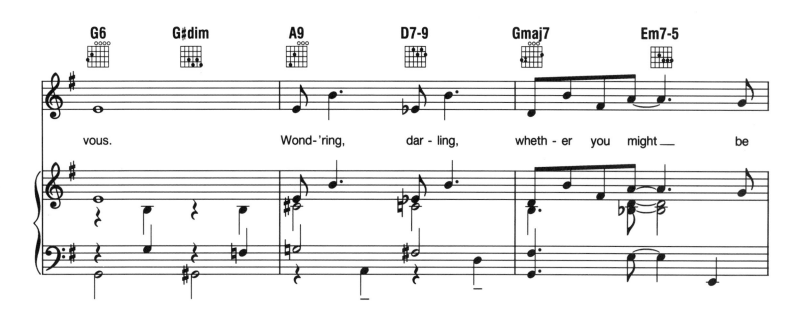

TRO - © Copyright 1914 and renewed 1942 and 1970 Cromwell Music, Inc., New York, NY
International Copyright Secured   Made in U.S.A.
Used by Permission

DOWNTOWN

Words and Music by TONY HATCH

Medium Rock

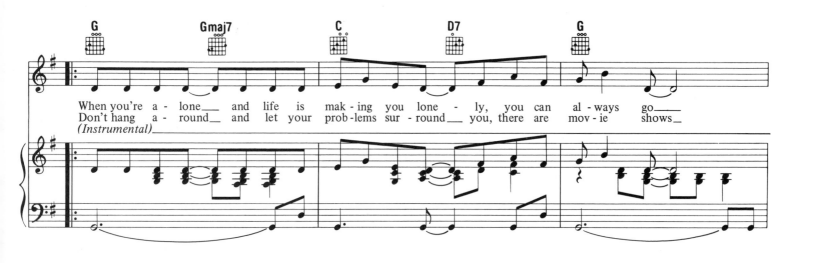

When you're a - lone___ and life is mak - ing you lone - ly, you can al - ways go___
Don't hang a - round___ and let your prob - lems sur - round___ you, there are mov - ie shows___
*(Instrumental)*___

down - town. When you've got wor - ries, all the noise and the hur - ry seems to
down - town. May - be you know___ some lit - tle plac - es to go___ to where they

© Copyright 1964 by Welbeck Music Ltd., London, England
Sole Selling Agent MCA Music, A Division of MCA Inc., New York, NY
International Copyright Secured   Made in U.S.A.   All Rights Reserved

MCA MUSIC

153

ENDLESS LOVE

Words and Music by
LIONEL RICHIE

Copyright © 1981 by PGP Music and Brockman Music
All rights administered by Intersong-USA throughout the world
International Copyright Secured   ALL RIGHTS RESERVED   Printed in the U.S.A.
Unauthorized copying, arranging, adapting, recording or public performance is an infringement of copyright.
Infringers are liable under the law.

From Walt Disney's "CINDERELLA"

A DREAM IS A WISH YOUR HEART MAKES

Words and Music by MACK DAVID,
AL HOFFMAN and JERRY LIVINGSTON

© 1948 WALT DISNEY MUSIC COMPANY
Copyright Renewed
International Copyright Secured   Made in U.S.A.   All Rights Reserved

EASY TO LOVE
(From "BORN TO LOVE")

Words and Music by COLE PORTER

Lyrics:
You'd be so eas-y to love, So eas-y to i-dol-ize, all oth-ers a-bove, So worth the yearn-ing for,_____ So swell to keep ev'-ry home fire burn-

Copyright © 1936 by Chappell & Co., Inc.
Copyright Renewed, Assigned to John F. Wharton, Trustee of the Cole Porter Musical & Literary Property Trusts
Chappell & Co., Inc., owner of publication and allied rights throughout the World.
International Copyright Secured   ALL RIGHTS RESERVED   Printed in the U.S.A.
Unauthorized copying, arranging, adapting, recording or public performance is an infringement of copyright.
Infringers are liable under the law.

EVERY BREATH YOU TAKE

Words and Music by STING

Copyright © 1983 Magnetic Publishing Ltd.
Published in the U.S.A. and Canada by Regatta Music, Inc.
Rights in the U.S.A. and Canada administered by Illegal Songs, Inc.
International Copyright Secured   Made in U.S.A.   All Rights Reserved

EVERYTHING'S COMING UP ROSES

(From "GYPSY")

Words by Stephen Sondheim
Music by Jule Styne

Copyright © 1959 by Norbeth Productions, Inc. and Stephen Sondheim
Williamson Music Co. and Stratford Music Corp. owners of publication and allied rights for the Western Hemisphere.   Chappell & Co., Inc., sole selling agent.
International Copyright Secured   ALL RIGHTS RESERVED   Printed in the U.S.A.
Unauthorized copying, arranging, adapting, recording or public performance is an infringement of copyright.
Infringers are liable under the law.

EVERYBODY LOVES MY BABY

(But My Baby Don't Love Nobody But Me)

Words and Music by JACK PALMER
and SPENCER WILLIAMS

With a beat

VERSE

I'm as hap-py as a king, ___ Feel-in' good 'n' ev-'ry-thing. ___ I'm just like a bird in Spring, ___

© Copyright 1924 by MCA MUSIC, A Division of MCA Inc., New York, NY
Copyright Renewed
International Copyright Secured   Made in U.S.A.   All Rights Reserved

MCA MUSIC

FALLING IN LOVE WITH LOVE

(From "THE BOYS FROM SYRACUSE")

Words by LORENZ HART
Music by RICHARD RODGERS

Copyright © 1938 by Chappell & Co., Inc.
Copyright Renewed.
International Copyright Secured   ALL RIGHTS RESERVED   Printed in the U.S.A.
Unauthorized copying, arranging, adapting, recording or public performance is an infringement of copyright.
Infringers are liable under the law.

FOR ALL WE KNOW
(From the Motion Picture "LOVERS AND OTHER STRANGERS")

Words by ROBB WILSON and JAMES GRIFFIN
Music by FRED KARLIN

Moderato, with a light beat

© Copyright 1970 by MUSIC CORPORATION OF AMERICA, INC., New York, NY
International Copyright Secured   Made in U.S.A.   All Rights Reserved
MCA MUSIC

A FINE ROMANCE

Words by DOROTHY FIELDS
Music by JEROME KERN

Copyright © 1936 T.B. Harms Company (c/o The Welk Music Group, Santa Monica, CA 90401)
Copyright renewed.
International Copyright Secured   Made in U.S.A.   All Rights Reserved

Interlude *(dialogue)*

(I Love You)
FOR SENTIMENTAL REASONS

Words by DEEK WATSON
Music by WILLIAM BEST

© Copyright 1945, 1946 by DUCHESS MUSIC CORPORATION, 445 Park Avenue, New York, NY
International Copyright Secured   Made in U.S.A.   All Rights Reserved

MCA MUSIC

FROM THIS MOMENT ON
(From "OUT OF THIS WORLD")

Words and Music by COLE PORTER

Moderately slow

Now that we are close, no more nights mor-ose, Now that we are one, the be-guine has just be-gun. Now that we're side by side, the fu-ture looks so gay, Now we are

Copyright © 1950 by Cole Porter
Copyright renewed, assigned to Robert H. Montgomery, Trustee of the Cole Porter Musical & Literary Property Trusts.   Chappell & Co., Inc., publisher.
International Copyright Secured   ALL RIGHTS RESERVED   Printed in the U.S.A.
Unauthorized copying, arranging, adapting, recording or public performance is an infringement of copyright.
Infringers are liable under the law.

FRIENDSHIP

Words and Music by COLE PORTER

Copyright © 1939 by Chappell & Co., Inc.
Copyright Renewed, Assigned to John F. Wharton, Trustee of the Cole Porter Musical & Literary Property Trusts
Chappell & Co., Inc., owner of the publication and allied rights throughout the World.
International Copyright Secured   ALL RIGHTS RESERVED   Printed in the U.S.A.
Unauthorized copying, arranging, adapting, recording or public performance is an infringement of copyright.
Infringers are liable under the law.

GET ME TO THE CHURCH ON TIME

(From "MY FAIR LADY")

Words by ALAN JAY LERNER
Music by FREDERICK LOEWE

Copyright © 1956 by Alan Jay Lerner and Frederick Loewe
Chappell & Co., Inc., owner of publication and allied rights throughout the World.
International Copyright Secured   ALL RIGHTS RESERVED   Printed in the U.S.A.
Unauthorized copying, arranging, adapting, recording or public performance is an infringement of copyright.
Infringers are liable under the law.

THE GIRL FROM IPANEMA
(Garôta De Ipanema)

Original Words by VINICIUS DE MORAES
English Words by NORMAN GIMBEL
Music by ANTONIO CARLOS JOBIM

Bossa Nova

© Copyright 1963 by Antonio Carlos Jobim and Vinicius De Moraes, Brazil
Sole Selling Agent DUCHESS MUSIC CORPORATION (MCA), New York, NY for all English Speaking Countries
International Copyright Secured   Made in U.S.A.   All Rights Reserved

MCA MUSIC

GETTING TO KNOW YOU

(From "THE KING AND I")

Words by OSCAR HAMMERSTEIN II
Music by RICHARD RODGERS

Copyright © 1951 by Richard Rodgers and Oscar Hammerstein II. Copyright Renewed.
Williamson Music Co., owner of publication and allied rights for all countries of the Western Hemisphere and Japan.
Chappell & Co., Inc., sole selling agent.
International Copyright Secured   ALL RIGHTS RESERVED   Printed in the U.S.A.
Unauthorized copying, arranging, adapting, recording or public performance is an infringement of copyright.
Infringers are liable under the law.

GOIN' OUT OF MY HEAD

Words and Music by TEDDY RANDAZZO
and BOBBY WEINSTEIN

Copyright © 1964 Vogue Music (c/o The Welk Music Group, Santa Monica, CA 90401)
International Copyright Secured   Made in U.S.A.   All Rights Reserved

GOODBYE YELLOW BRICK ROAD

Words and Music by ELTON JOHN
and BERNIE TAUPIN

Moderately slow, in 2

Copyright © 1973 DICK JAMES MUSIC LIMITED, James House, 5 Theobald's Rd., London WC1X 8SE, England
All rights for the United States of America and Canada controlled by DICK JAMES MUSIC, INC., 24 Music Square East, Nashville, TN 37203
International Copyright Secured   Made in U.S.A.   All Rights Reserved

GONNA BUILD A MOUNTAIN

(From the Musical Production "STOP THE WORLD — I WANT TO GET OFF")

Words and Music by
LESLIE BRICUSSE
and ANTHONY NEWLEY

© Copyright 1961 TRO Essex Music Ltd., London, England
TRO - Ludlow Music, Inc., New York, controls all publication rights for the U.S.A. and Canada
International Copyright Secured   Made in U.S.A.
All Rights Reserved Including Public Performance For Profit
Used by Permission

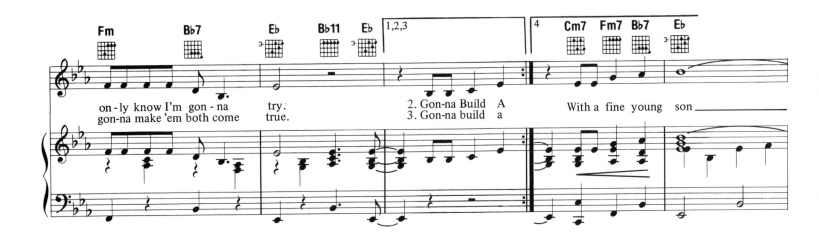

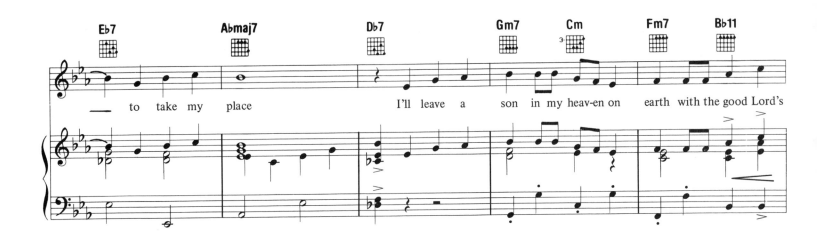

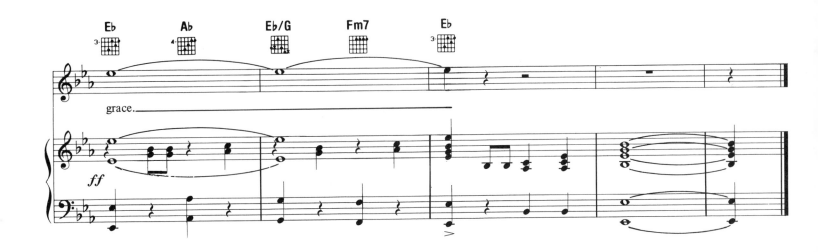

Verse 3. Gon-na build a heaven from a little hell.
Gon-na build a heaven and I know darn well.
If I build my mountain with a lot of care.
And take my daydream up the mountain heaven
will be waiting there.

Verse 4. When I've built that heaven as I will some day
And the Lord sends Gabriel to take me away,
Wanna fine young son to take my place
I'll leave a son in my heav-en on earth,
With the Lord's good grace.

GREEN GREEN GRASS OF HOME

Words and Music by CURLY PUTMAN

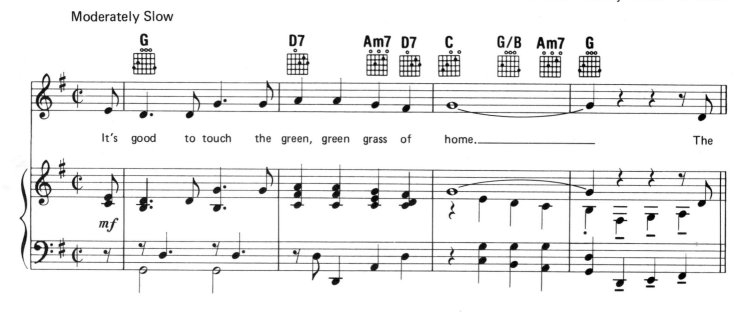

It's good to touch the green, green grass of home._____ The

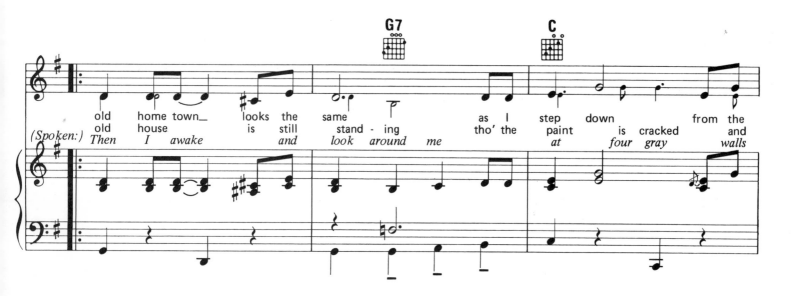

old home town___ looks the same as I step down from the
old house is still standing tho' the paint is cracked and

(Spoken:) Then I awake and look around me at four gray walls

train,_____ and there to meet me is my ma - ma___ and
dry,_____ and there's that old oak tree that I used___ to
that surround me and I realize that I was only dreaming.

Copyright © 1965 by Tree Publishing Co., Inc. 8 Music Square West, Nashville, TN 37203
This arrangement Copyright © 1984 by Tree Publishing Co., Inc.
International Copyright Secured   Made in U.S.A.   All Rights Reserved

THE HAWAIIAN WEDDING SONG

English Words by AL HOFFMAN & DICK MANNING
Hawaiian Words & Music by CHARLES E. KING

Slowly, with much warmth

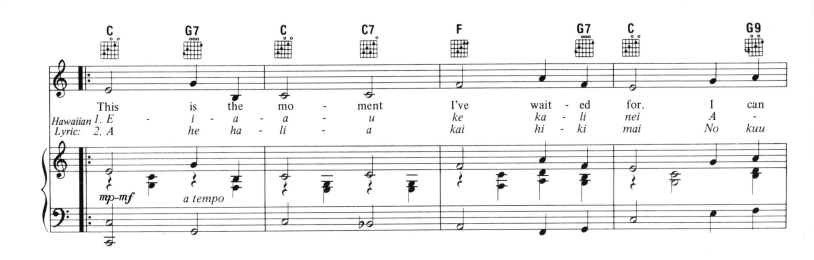

This is the mo - ment I've wait - ed for. I can
Hawaiian 1. E - i - a - a - u ke ka - li nei A -
Lyric: 2. A he ha - li - a kai hi - ki mai No kuu

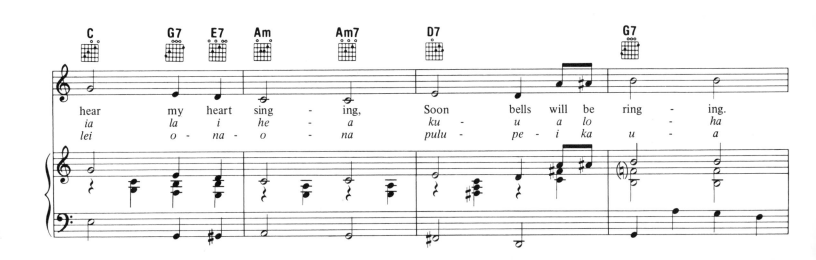

hear my heart sing - ing, Soon bells will be ring - ing.
ia la i he - a ku - u a lo - ha
lei o - na - o - na pulu - pe - i ka u - a

© Copyright 1926, 1958 by Charles E. King Music Co., L.I. New York
Sole Selling Agent MCA MUSIC, a division of MCA Inc., New York, N.Y. for U.S.A. and Canada
International Copyright Secured   Made in U.S.A.   All Rights Reserved

MCA MUSIC

HAVE I TOLD YOU LATELY THAT I LOVE YOU

Words and Music by SCOTT WISEMAN

With movement

Have I told you late - ly that I love you? _____ Could I
told you late - ly how I miss you? _____ When the
told you late - ly when I'm sleep - ing? _____ Ev - 'ry

tell you once a - gain some - how. _____ Have I told with
stars are shin - ing in the sky. _____ Have I told you
dream I dream is you some - how. _____ Have I told you

all my heart and soul how I a - dore you? Well dar - ling, I'm tell - ing you
why the nights are long when you're not with me? Well dar - ling, I'm tell - ing you
who I'd like to share my love for - ev - er? Well dar - ling, I'm tell - ing you

© Copyright 1945, 1946 by Duchess Music Corporation, New York, NY. Copyright renewed
Rights administered by MCA Music, A Division of MCA Inc., New York, NY
International Copyright Secured   Made in U.S.A.   All Rights Reserved

MCA MUSIC

HEARTACHES

Words by JOHN KLENNER
Music by AL HOFFMAN

© Copyright 1931, 1942 by MCA MUSIC, A Division of MCA Inc., New York, NY
Copyright Renewed
International Copyright Secured   Made in U.S.A.   All Rights Reserved

MCA MUSIC

227

HEARTACHES BY THE NUMBER

By HARLAN HOWARD

Copyright © 1959 by Tree Publishing Co., Inc., 8 Music Square West, Nashville, TN 37203
This arrangement Copyright © 1984 by Tree Publishing Co., Inc.
International Copyright Secured   Made in U.S.A.   All Rights Reserved

CHORUS

Now I've got heart-aches by the num-ber, trou-bles by the score. Ev'-ry day you

love me less, each day I love you more. Yes, I've got heart-aches by the num-ber,___ a

love that I can't win, but the day that I stop count-ing, that's the day my world will

end._____ day my world will end._____

HEARTLIGHT

Words and Music by NEIL DIAMOND,
BURT BACHARACH and CAROLE BAYER SAGER

Light Rock Ballad

Come back a - gain.

I want you to stay _ next time, _

'cause some - times the world ain't kind _ when

© 1982 STONEBRIDGE MUSIC, NEW HIDDEN VALLEY MUSIC and CAROLE BAYER SAGER MUSIC
All Rights Reserved

E♭maj9 Gm7 Fm7 A♭/B♭
3
And home is the most ex - cel - lent
E♭maj7 Cm7 Fm7 Fm7/B♭ Gm/B♭ A♭/B♭ Gm/B♭
place of all. And I'll be right here if you should call me.
D.S. al Coda
Turn on your
mf
CODA
E♭maj9 A♭ A♭/B♭ B♭7 E♭
you and me.
p
A♭ A♭/B♭ B♭7 E♭ A♭ A♭/B♭ B♭7 E♭
Turn on your heart - light now, Turn on your heart - light now.
pp rit.

HELLO AGAIN
(From the motion picture THE JAZZ SINGER)

Words by NEIL DIAMOND
Music by NEIL DIAMOND and ALAN LINDGREN

Moderately slow

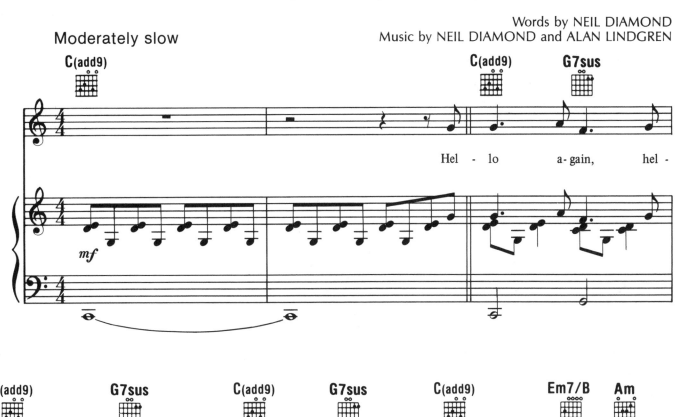

Hel - lo a - gain, hel -

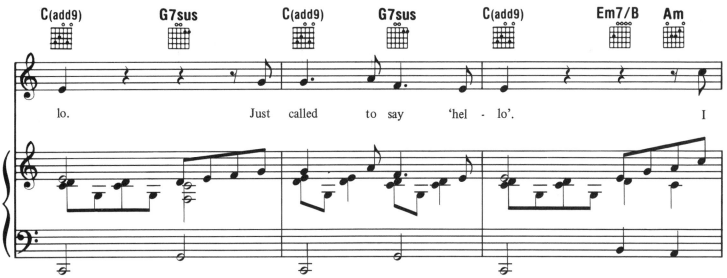

lo.   Just called to say 'hel - lo'.   I

could - n't sleep at all to - night. And I know it's late, but I

© 1980 Stonebridge Music
All Rights Reserved

HELLO, YOUNG LOVERS
(From "THE KING AND I")

Words by OSCAR HAMMERSTEIN II
Music by RICHARD RODGERS

Very moderately

Copyright © 1951 by Richard Rodgers and Oscar Hammerstein II. Copyright Renewed.
Williamson Music Co., owner of publication and allied rights for all countries of the Western Hemisphere and Japan.
Chappell & Co., Inc. sole selling agent.
International Copyright Secured   ALL RIGHTS RESERVED   Printed in the U.S.A.
Unauthorized copying, arranging, adapting, recording or public performance is an infringement of copyright.
Infringers are liable under the law.

HERE COMES THAT RAINY DAY FEELING AGAIN

Words and Music by TONY MACAULAY,
ROGER COOK and ROGER GREENAWAY

Copyright © 1970 COOKAWAY MUSIC LTD.
Copyright assigned 1981 to DICK JAMES MUSIC LTD., James House, 5 Theobald's Rd., London WC1X 8SE, England
All rights for the United States and Canada controlled by DEJAMUS, INC., 24 Music Square East, Nashville, TN 37203
International Copyright Secured   Made in U.S.A.   All Rights Reserved

HOW ARE THINGS IN GLOCCA MORRA

(From "FINIAN'S RAINBOW")

Words by E.Y. HARBURG
Music by BURTON LANE

Slowly

Copyright © 1946 by The Players Music Corp.
Copyright Renewed, Assigned to Chappell & Co., Inc.
International Copyright Secured   ALL RIGHTS RESERVED   Printed in the U.S.A.
Unauthorized copying, arranging, adapting, recording or public performance is an infringement of copyright.
Infringers are liable under the law.

I AM . . . I SAID

Words and Music by NEIL DIAMOND

© 1971 PROPHET MUSIC, INC.
All Rights Reserved

HOW INSENSITIVE

Original Words by VINICIUS DE MORAES
English Words by NORMAN GIMBEL
Music by ANTONIO CARLOS JOBIM

© Copyright 1963, 1964 by Antonio Carlos Jobim and Vinicius De Moraes, Brazil
Sole Selling Agent DUCHESS MUSIC CORPORATION (MCA), New York, NY for the U.S.A. and Canada
International Copyright Secured   Made in U.S.A.   All Rights Reserved

MCA MUSIC

I CAN'T GET STARTED
From "ZIEGFIELD FOLLIES OF 1936"

Words by IRA GERSHWIN
Music by VERNON DUKE

Copyright © 1935 by Chappell & Co., Inc.
Copyright Renewed
International Copyright Secured   ALL RIGHTS RESERVED   Printed in the U.S.A.
Unauthorized copying, arranging, adapting, recording or public performance is an infringement of copyright.
Infringers are liable under the law.

I CONCENTRATE ON YOU

Words and Music by
COLE PORTER

Copyright © 1939 by Chappell & Co., Inc.
Copyright Renewed, Assigned to John F. Wharton, Trustee of the Cole Porter Musical & Literary Property Trusts
Chappell & Co., Inc., owner of publication and allied rights throughout the World.
International Copyright Secured   ALL RIGHTS RESERVED   Printed in the U.S.A.
Unauthorized copying, arranging, adapting, recording or public performance is an infringement of copyright.
Infringers are liable under the law.

I COULD HAVE DANCED ALL NIGHT
(From "MY FAIR LADY")

Words by ALAN JAY LERNER
Music by FREDERICK LOEWE

Copyright © 1956 by Alan Jay Lerner & Frederick Loewe   Copyright Renewed
Chappell & Co., Inc., owner of publication and allied rights throughout the world.
International Copyright Secured   ALL RIGHTS RESERVED   Printed in the U.S.A.
Unauthorized copying, arranging, adapting, recording or public performance is an infringement of copyright.
Infringers are liable under the law.

I DON'T CARE IF THE SUN DON'T SHINE

Words and Music by MACK DAVID

Copyright © 1950 Harry Von Tilzer Music Publishing Company (c/o the Welk Music Group, Santa Monica, CA 90401) Copyright renewed.
International Copyright Secured   Made in U.S.A.   All Rights Reserved

I CRIED FOR YOU

Words and Music by ARTHUR FREED,
GUS ARNHEIM and ABE LYMAN

Copyright © 1923 ARTHUR FREED MUSIC
Pursuant to Sections 304(c) and 401(b) of the U.S. Copyright Law.
International Copyright Secured   All Rights Reserved

269

I DON'T KNOW HOW TO LOVE HIM

(From "JESUS CHRIST SUPERSTAR")

Words by TIM RICE
Music by ANDREW LLOYD WEBBER

Slowly, tenderly and very expressively

© Copyright 1970 by LEEDS MUSIC LTD., London, England
Sole Selling Agent LEEDS MUSIC CORPORATION (MCA), New York, NY for North, South and Central America
International Copyright Secured   Made in U.S.A.   All Rights Reserved

MCA MUSIC

271

I DON'T WANT TO SET THE WORLD ON FIRE

Words by EDDIE SEILER and SOL MARCUS
Music by BENNIE BENJAMIN and EDDIE DURHAM

© 1940, 1941 CHERIO CORP.
© Renewed 1968, 1969 CHERIO CORP.
International Copyright Secured   Made in U.S.A.   All Rights Reserved

I ENJOY BEING A GIRL
(From "FLOWER DRUM SONG")

Words by OSCAR HAMMERSTEIN II
Music by RICHARD RODGERS

Copyright © 1958 by Richard Rodgers and Oscar Hammerstein II.
Williamson Music Co., owner of publication and allied rights for all countries of the Western Hemisphere and Japan.
Chappell & Co., Inc., sole selling agent.
International Copyright Secured   ALL RIGHTS RESERVED   Printed in the U.S.A.
Unauthorized copying, arranging, adapting, recording or public performance is an infringement of copyright.
Infringers are liable under the law.

I GUESS THAT'S WHY THEY CALL IT THE BLUES

Words and Music by
ELTON JOHN, BERNIE TAUPIN
and DAVEY JOHNSTONE

Copyright © 1983 by Big Pig Music Ltd.
Published in the U.S.A. by Intersong-USA, Inc.
International Copyright Secured   ALL RIGHTS RESERVED   Printed in the U.S.A.
Unauthorized copying, arranging, adapting, recording or public performance is an infringement of copyright.
Infringers are liable under the law.

I HAVE DREAMED
(From "THE KING AND I")

Words by Oscar Hammerstein II
Music by Richard Rodgers

Copyright © 1951 by Richard Rodgers and Oscar Hammerstein II. Copyright Renewed.
Williamson Music Co., owner of publication and allied rights for all countries of the Western Hemisphere and Japan.
Chappell & Co., Inc., sole selling agent.
International Copyright Secured   ALL RIGHTS RESERVED   Printed in the U.S.A.
Unauthorized copying, arranging, adapting, recording or public performance is an infringement of copyright.
Infringers are liable under the law.

I LOVE PARIS
(From "CAN-CAN")

Words and Music by COLE PORTER

Copyright © 1953 by Cole Porter
Copyright renewed, assigned to Robert H. Montgomery, Trustee of the Cole Porter Musical and Literary Property Trusts.
Chappell & Co., Inc., Publisher
International Copyright Secured   ALL RIGHTS RESERVED   Printed in the U.S.A.
Unauthorized copying, arranging, adapting, recording or public performance is an infringement of copyright.
Infringers are liable under the law.

Piano/Vocal MIXED FOLIOS
Presenting the best variety of piano/vocal folios. Music includes guitar chord frames.

BEST BROADWAY SONGS EVER 00309155
Over 70 tunes featuring: All The Things You Are • Bewitched • Don't Cry For Me Argentina • I Could Have Danced All Night • If Ever I Would Leave You • Memory • Ol' Man River • You'll Never Walk Alone • and many more.

BEST CONTEMPORARY SONGS — 50 Top Hits 00359190
Some of the best, most recent hits, featuring: Any Day Now • Deja Vu • Endless Love • Flashdance...What A Feeling • I.O.U. • Islands In The Stream • September Morn • Through The Years • You Needed Me • and many more.

THE BEST COUNTRY SONGS EVER 00359498
79 all-time country hits including: Always On My Mind • Could I Have This Dance • God Bless The U.S.A. • Help Me Make It Through The Night • Islands In The Stream • and many more.

THE BEST EASY LISTENING SONGS EVER 00359193
Over 100 beautiful songs including: Around The World • Candle On The Water • Day By Day • A Foggy Day • I'll Never Smile Again • Just In Time • Manhattan • Strangers In The Night • and many more.

BEST KNOWN LATIN SONGS 00359194
A fabulous selection of over 50 favorite Latin songs including: Blame It On The Bossa Nova • A Day In The Life Of A Fool • The Girl From Ipanema • Poinciana • Quando, Quando, Quando • Spanish Eyes • Watch What Happens • Yellow Days • and many more!

THE BEST SONGS EVER 00359224
75 all-time hits including: Climb Ev'ry Mountain • Edelweiss • Feelings • Here's That Rainy Day • I Left My Heart In San Francisco • Love Is Blue • People • Stardust • Sunrise, Sunset • Woman In Love • many more.

THE BEST STANDARDS EVER Volume 1 00359231
and Volume 2 00359232
A two volume collection of 140 vintage and contemporary standards including: All The Things You Are • Endless Love • The Hawaiian Wedding Song • I Left My Heart In San Francisco • Misty • My Way • Old Cape Cod • People • Wish You Were Here • Yesterday's Songs • and many more.

THE BIG BAND ERA 00359260
Over 90 top songs from the time of the big bands including: Harbor Lights • I Can't Get Started • In The Mood • Juke Box Saturday Night • Moonglow • Paper Doll • String Of Pearls • Tuxedo Junction • Amapola • Jersey Bounce • and many more.

THE BIG 80 SONGBOOK 00359265
80 Recent hits and favorite standards including: Autumn Leaves • Can't Smile Without You • Ebony And Ivory • Midnight Cowboy • More • Riders In The Sky • Sentimental Journey • She Touched Me • Stormy Weather • You Don't Bring Me Flowers • and much more.

BROADWAY DELUXE 00309245
126 Smash Broadway songs including: Cabaret • Edelweiss • I Could Have Danced All Night • Memory • Send In The Clowns • Seventy Six Trombones • Sunrise, Sunset • Try To Remember • What Kind Of Fool Am I? • A Wonderful Guy • and many, more.

CONTEMPORARY HIT DUETS 00359501
14 hit duets from today's biggest pop stars includes Don't Go Breaking My Heart • Endless Love • Ebony And Ivory • Say, Say, Say • You Don't Bring Me Flowers • and more.

CONTEMPORARY LOVE SONGS 00359496
A collection of today's best love songs including Endless Love • September Morn • Feelings • Through The Years • and more.

80's GOLD UPDATE 00359740
Over 70 Hits from the 80's including: All Through The Night • Endless Love • Every Breath You Take • Fortress Around Your Heart • Memory • Miami Vice • One Night In Bangkok • Sentimental Street • What's Love Got To Do With It • Total Eclipse Of The Heart • and more!

FAVORITE HAWAIIAN SONGS 00359852
30 island favorites including Aloha Oe • One Paddle, Two Paddle • Red Sails In The Sunset • Tiny Bubbles • and many more.

GOLDEN ENCYCLOPEDIA OF FOLK MUSIC 00359905
A giant collection of more than 180 classic folk songs including songs of true love, unrequited and false love, spirituals, songs of the west, jolly reunions, international songs and singing the blues.

GRANDMA MOSES SONGBOOK 00359938
A beautiful collection of over 80 traditional and folk songs highlighted by the fascinating paintings of Grandma Moses. Features: America The Beautiful • The Glow Worm • Honeysuckle Rose • I'll Be Home On Christmas Day • Look To The Rainbow • Suddenly There's A Valley • Sunrise, Sunset • Try To Remember • and many, many more!

No. 1 SONGS OF THE 80's 00310666
Arthur's Theme • Everything She Wants • Everytime You Go Away • Careless Whisper • Sailing • What's Love Got To Do With It • The Reflex • Time After Time • and more.

#1 SONGS FROM THE 70's & 80's 00310665
60 of the top songs from the Billboard Hot 100 charts of the 70's and 80's, featuring: Every Breath You Take • How Deep Is Your Love • Joy To The World • Laughter In The Rain • Love Will Keep Us Together • Love's Theme • Maneater • Maniac • Morning Train • Stayin' Alive • and more.

150 OF THE MOST BEAUTIFUL SONGS EVER
Perfect Bound - 00360735   Plastic Comb Bound - 00360734
Bali Ha'i • Bewitched • Could I Have This Dance • I Remember It Well • I'll Be Seeing You • If I Ruled The World • Love Is Blue • Memory • Songbird • When I Need You • and more.

ROCK ON! 00360932
A collection of 50 top rock hits spanning the decades from the 60's to the present. Includes such rock classics as Free Bird • A Whiter Shade Of Pale • Sunshine Of Your Love • Maggie May • and many, many more.

70 CONTEMPORARY HITS 00361056
A super collection of 70 hits featuring: Every Breath You Take • Time After Time • Memory • Wake Me Up Before You Go-Go • Endless Love • Islands In The Stream • Through The Years • Valotte • and many more.

23 AWARD WINNNG POP HITS 00361385
23 of the best including Don't Cry Out Loud • Flashdance...What A Feeling • Memory • You Needed Me • and more.

VIDEO ROCK HITS 00361456
A collection of hits by today's biggest video artists — Cindy Lauper, Twisted Sister, Tina Turner, Wham! and others. 21 songs including: Careless Whisper • Hungry Like The Wolf • She Bop • What's Love Got To Do With It • and many more.

YOUNG AT HEART SONGBOOK 00361820
101 light hearted, fun loving favorites: Alley Cat • Bandstand Boogie • Bye Bye Blues • Five Foot Two, Eyes Of Blue • I Could Have Danced All Night • Let Me Entertain You • The Sound Of Music • Tiny Bubbles • True Love • Young At Heart • and more.

ALSO AVAILABLE...

HAL LEONARD CHARTBUSTER SERIES
frequently released books of chart songs which include the top recorded hits from Billboard's Top 100 Chart.

PIANO ALPHABETICAL SONGFINDER 72000004
Complete listing of the thousands of songs included in the Easy Piano and Piano/Vocal/Guitar books. Song titles are cross-referenced to the books in which they can be found. Available free of charge from your local music store. Or, write to:
HAL LEONARD PUBLISHING CORP.
P.O. Box 13819, Milwaukee, WI 53213

For more information, contact your local music dealer, or write directly to:

HAL LEONARD PUBLISHING CORPORATION
8112 West Bluemound Rd. P.O. Box 13819 Milwaukee, WI 53213